WAY TO GO

SONGS FOR BABY BOOMER GOODBYES

JAY SNYDER

Concept and execution: Jay Snyder

Editor: Dan Marcus
Cover & Graphics: Maxine Cameron
Publisher: Golden Retriever Media

Other Books by Jay Snyder

Parisian Reasons:
An Homage to Hemingway's A Moveable Feast
•
Retro Sketches:
A Musical Director Remembers
•
Piano Fundamentals:
Piano and Fundamentals for Everyone, Vols. 1 & 2

❀ INTRO ❀

When you're a lifelong musician people expect you to know every popular song ever written. That's especially true if you're a musical director which I was. Once, while sitting at the piano, someone came up to me and said, "I have a request. Play 'Short Johnnie's My Doctor.'" I laughed because the title was funny and asked, "Who did that?" "Dinah Washington," came the reply. "It's a B side."

And if you know a little Bach or Beethoven and taught music in college, you're also expected to know every classical piece ever written. "How does the third movement of the Fourth Symphony by Sibelius go?" they'd ask. "I thought Sibelius wrote a music notation program?" I'd answer. "Well, if you don't know that, can you whistle the finale to Finlandia?"

Along with a career in music, I was first and foremost a baby boomer, the owner of an aqua-colored transistor radio and a collection of LPs and singles. The tunes from just before, during, and after Beatlemania are in my blood so those are the songs and melodies I'm using for this book with a few exceptions. My list is not meant to be exhaustive but it contains some relevant material and serves the situation we've set up for ourselves: choose some fitting music for a friend's final goodbye.

You have many options as far as the mood you set: contemplative, morose, ironic, sentimental, uplifting, gracious, forgiving, and peaceful for what has become known as a "celebration of life." Choose one piece of music or several. Within these 100 memories you're sure to find just the right ones.

Table of Contents / Boomer Categories

Table of Contents / Boomer Categories, continued

Table of Contents / Boomer Categories, continued

ABSURD with a message

❀ **FEELING GOOD** – *Nina Simone*
This life-affirming song comes from the musical *The Roar of the Greasepaint, the Smell of the Crowd*. A feel-good song for a feel-bad day.

❀ **I CAN SEE CLEARLY NOW** – *Johnny Nash*
Maybe the departed can see clearly now or maybe they can't. Only those with faith know with certainty.

❀ **THE LAST TIME** – *The Rolling Stones*
Got irony if you want it.

❀ **TIME WON'T LET ME** – *The Outsiders*
Goodbyes don't always have to be sad affairs. A foot-tapping opening number could possibly change the mood from bad to tolerable. Fade the track during the guitar solo and cue the speaker unless you have a room full of guitar players.

❀ **TIRED OF WAITING FOR YOU** – *The Kinks*
The situation proves the idea of the song: someone waited too long.

❀ **YOU'VE LET YOURSELF GO** – *Charles Aznavour*
Some might take offense but whimsical for the right crowd.

ALBINO

❀ **A WHITER SHADE OF PALE** – *Procol Harum*
A song to memorialize the very white and those who embraced SPF numbers above 80. Organ lends a traditional touch.

BIKER

✿ **BABA O'RILEY** – *The Who*
For independent thinkers and the rebellious.

✿ **BORN TO BE WILD** – *Steppenwolf*
If your friend was a biker or biker chick, please don't use this song. Surely there's something less obvious. However, if we're talking about weekend Harley warriors such as accountants, dentists, florists, or Zamboni operators then bring it on.

✿ **ROCK AND ROLL, PART 2** – *Gary Glitter*
There's only one word (interjection, really) in this song sung over and over: "Hey," leaving room for many interpretations.

✿ **WILD WEEKEND** – *The Rebels*
If the big event is held on a weekend and you were a hog fan, this 1963 hit is for you if you've rejected the overused "Born to be Wild."

CAGE-FREE HUSBANDS

❀ **ALL RIGHT NOW** – *Free*

As no wife in her right mind would allow her mate to use this chauvinist anthem at his sendoff, it would be necessary for henpecked hubby to make prearrangements: an edited CD or file sent off on a wing and a prayer.

CONTRITE

✿ **I'M SORRY** – *Brenda Lee*

Living an entire life as an S.O.B. but seeing the light is always possible. He was a substance abuser of some kind, took money from the needy, didn't really work, but in the end realized the error of his ways.

COVETOUS

✿ **MONEY (That's What I Want)** – *Barrett Strong*
She was grabby. Everyone knew it and talked about her
cheapness behind her back. But a fat bank account was much
more important than what people thought. Look at that
chunk of ice on her finger. She did take it with her!

COWGIRL

❀ **WILDFIRE** – *Michael Martin Murphey*
Teachers of literature and songwriting caution, "Avoid senti-mentalism." Okay, but here's a hit record dripping as it exits the sauna of sentiment. Use this song for a woman who was an individualist and rode a horse.

DRUGGIE

❀ **WHITE RABBIT** – *Jefferson Airplane*
Author Lewis Carroll became associated with hallucinogens in the '60s by writing "Alice in Wonderland." Set to a bolero beat and sung by Grace Slick with restraint, then no restraint; anyone who — sad to say — OD'd on acid, mushrooms, or elephant tranquilizer now has an appropriate sendoff.

ENTERTAINER

❀ **SAM, THE OLD ACCORDION MAN** –
The Williams Sisters
Although the character in the song plays accordion, it's easy
to imagine anyone who loves to entertain having this piece
played to capture an enjoyable part of their life.

EXISTENTIALIST

❀ **CAST YOUR FATE TO THE WIND** – *Sounds Orchestral*
A beautiful instrumental to be played in the background if
you're scattering ashes.

❀ **IS THAT ALL THERE IS** – *Peggy Lee*
Peggy Lee is linked forever with the song "Fever."
It's a good song. She sang it convincingly and it's easy to play.
Four chords. But "Is That All There Is" is deeper – describing
a young girl observing a circus with detachment. Then her
house burns down and she's mysteriously cool about that.
Years later she loses her groovy guy of 1969 but takes it all in
stride, sensing his long sideburns will soon be out of style.

*For the person who viewed life as just a bowl of desiccated
cherries.*

FEMINIST

✿ **THESE BOOTS ARE MADE FOR WALKIN'** –
Nancy Sinatra
Ms. X didn't necessarily have to have been a feminist; she could have just exploded onto the scene as an assertive, affirmative daughter of the '60s. But she'd be happy you chose a song that contains some of the D.N.A. of the Women's Movement.

GRANDIOSE

❀ **2001: ALSO SPRACH ZARATHUSTRA** –
Berlin Philharmonic
These days few people, including me, know who Zarathustra was, what he sprached, or what he stood for. Yet these thirty-two bars of music by Richard Strauss still live on. Why? The short answer is that filmmaker Stanley Kubrick chose it as the main title of *2001: A Space Odyssey,* and Elvis then used the melody to open his later shows.

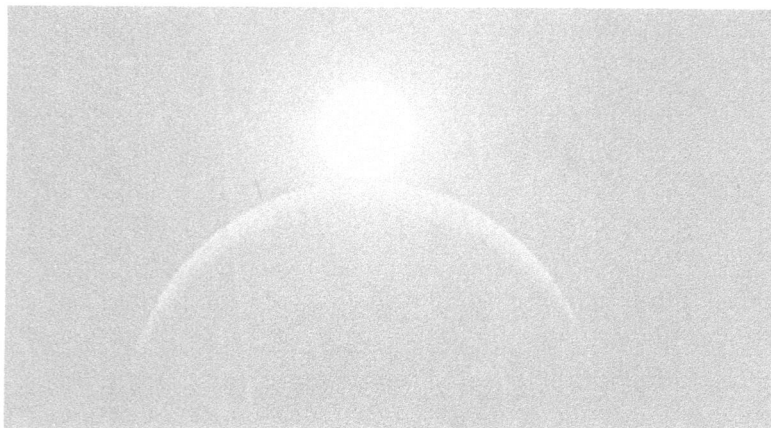

HE'S GONE

❀ **MY LOVE IS ALIVE** – *Gary Wright*
Somewhere, somehow they'll be reunited.

❀ **UNTIL IT'S TIME FOR YOU TO GO** – *Buffy Sainte-Marie*
Sums up precious days and nights together.

HIPPIE BOY

❀ **LET'S SPEND THE NIGHT TOGETHER** –
The Rolling Stones
The core, the pith, the thrust of popular music through the
ages has been — as Mick and Keith so eloquently put it —
"Let's spend the night together." Nothing more, nothing less
for hierophants, hermetics, and hormonal hippies.

HIPPIE GIRL

❀ **RUBY TUESDAY** – *The Rolling Stones*
She meant well but skipped out on the light bill.

❀ **SUZANNE** – *Leonard Cohen, Judy Collins*
Sacred in a secular way. To choose this song is to honor many.

❀ **WINDY** – *The Association*
I don't know why she bent over showing me her rainbow-
colored underwear, but Windy captured the essence of the
carefree, female side of the groovy '60s.

HUMANIST

✾ **BECAUSE** – *The Beatles*
In the words, melody, and arrangement live a marvelous
sense of wonderment and appreciation of the world.

IDEALISTIC

❀ **LOVE IS ALL AROUND** – *The Troggs*
The Beatles weren't the only ones who espoused love as the big idea, the unifying principle of the universe.

❀ **SMILE OF THE BEYOND** – *Mahavishnu Orchestra*
The voice of a sweet, sincere soprano backed with strings sings of what may be. Go from 0:00 to 2:50

INCARCERATED

✿ **I SHOT THE SHERIFF** – *Bob Marley and the Wailers*
For those wrongfully or rightfully confined who have now
forever flown the coop.

✿ **YOU'RE NO GOOD** – *Linda Ronstadt*
When any of the jailed financial minds from the debacle of
2008 reach the end of the line, let the many stockholders
who suffered stand arm in arm 'round the penitentiary singing
the words to this chorus. Or forgive and forget this song.

IRONIC

❀ **STAYIN' ALIVE** – *The Bee Gees, Darlene and Jonathan*
If you and your friends are daring enough to use "Stayin'
Alive" at a memorial service then you might want to consider
another version.

*Respected singer Jo Stafford and her bandleader husband, Paul
Weston had an underground act called Darlene and Jonathan.
She intentionally sang out of tune and the music tracks sound
like a vengeful audio editor went a-chopping. The results are not
to be believed.*

LIGHT-HEARTED

❀ **WONDERFUL COPENHAGEN** – *Connie Stevens*
Overproduction in this case has its place if the breaved
understand the music's intent: to cheer people up instead
of bringing them down. This charming piece of exploitation
is memorable if only for the American pronunciation of
Co-pen-hay-gen.

❀ **LOVIN' YOU** – *Minnie Riperton*
A song as light as air. Peaceful. Birds chirp. Feels like a
sunny day.

MARIJUANA ADVOCATE

❀ **LET'S GO GET STONED** – *Ray Charles*
Brother Ray nails escapism. Suitable for after the service, too.

❀ **RAINY DAY WOMEN #12 & 35** – *Bob Dylan*
No rain nor women but you probably know this song by its refrain "Everybody Must Get Stoned."

MISCREANT - HATER OF MAN

❀ **DON'T BOTHER ME** – *The Beatles*
Okay, George Harrison was not a hater of man; he was a lover of man but in 1963 it does sound like he wanted to at least be left alone. Maybe because — according to Beatle history — John and Paul conspired to help him not. Nevertheless, George was on his way to becoming a very good songwriter ("Something"). Here, in his artistic infancy, he gives us an appropriate song for agnostics, shut-ins, and put-upon rock stars.

❀ **GET OFF OF MY CLOUD** – *The Rolling Stones*
Done with the din.

❀ **I AM A ROCK** – *Simon and Garfunkle*
Paul Simon captured the fifteen-year-old mindset beautifully. If isolation haunted your friend like the bogeyman, or loneliness was always a piece of the puzzle, then take your troubles to Simon and Garfunkle.

❀ **LET ME BE** – *The Turtles*
You're a teenager. Your parents don't know anything. You went to your room, closed the door, and put on this record. No pre-fab destiny for you.

As one of your contemporaries passes out of this dimension, you choose this same song, still relevant, now a tribute.

NOBLE

❀ **BLAZING SADDLES** –
Frankie Laine (with the John Morris Orchestra)
As with the "Theme from Shaft" there is a sense of dignity
and justice in this song, but it's also funny so you'll need a
certain kind of crowd to appreciate this.

❀ **THEME FROM "ADVENTURES OF SUPERMAN"** –
Hollywood studio musicians
A march that rivals anything by John Philip Sousa. If they
found a red Superman cape in your friend's basement or
hiding place, you've also found one of his favorite triumphant
melodies.

❀ **THEME FROM SHAFT** – *Isaac Hayes*
It doesn't have the heft of the main theme from *2001* (Also
Spake You-Know-Who and his 100 piece orchestra) and it
shouldn't; it should be cool like your friend and it is.

❀ **TIME PASSED AUTUMN, PT.1** – *Claus Ogerman Orchestra*
The most subtle of these "noble" selections. Start at 0:00 and
stop at 0:50.

NON-ACCEPTANCE

❀ **BLACK IS BLACK** – *Los Bravos*
If you're familiar with the research of Elizabeth Kübler-Ross you know there are five stages of grief: denial, anger, bargaining, depression, and acceptance. Here, the singer embraces both denial and depression.

OUTSIDER

✿ **GRINNIN' IN YOUR FACE** – *Son House*
Maybe your friend experienced this lesson in life: "Just as soon as your back are turned/ they be tryin' to crush you down." People should know.

✿ **GYMNOPÉDIE No. 1** – *Various artists*
What can you say about Erik Satie, a composer from the French Impressionist period who wrote a suite for piano titled "Three Pieces in the Shape of a Pear"? Claude Debussy befriended him and enjoyed his music, but Satie, like Van Gogh, was not appreciated in his lifetime, viewed as somewhat of a kook. Too bad. His music is delicate, charming, and lives on.

If you knew someone who didn't really fit in, consider one of these three miniatures from the Gymnopédie suite – the first piece being the most familiar. Written and normally performed for solo piano, it has also been orchestrated by Debussy and others.

PARTIER

❀ **SWEET HOME ALABAMA** – *Lynyrd Skynyrd*
"Hello, my name is Jim Beam and I'll be your waiter this evening."

PEACEFUL

❀ **CHOPIN NOCTURNE No. 19 in E MINOR –**
Vitalij Margulis
The trouble with nocturnes is that they're so soothing they can put you to sleep — embarrassing at a memorial service. The trick, then, is to select a piece or part of a piece that won't have a somnambulistic effect.

The one I've chosen is tranquil but less so than a capful of NyQuil. I've experimented on myself and find that exactly a minute and fifty seconds is the correct amount of Chopin.

PERSEVERANT

❀ **THEME FROM JEAN DE FLORETTE** –
Various European Orchestras
Derived in part from Verdi's *La Fuerza del Destino*, this
haunting melody played on harmonica with strings in the
background was written for a character who never gave up
but lost in the end — unless you feel that by simply trying,
one never loses.

❀ **WHIP IT** – *Devo*
Not necessarily a song to lay a dominatrix to rest; it's all
about overcoming overwhelming odds. So if a dream was
realized or a life was lived pursuing it, why not use this song?

POIGNANT

❀ **AZULÃO** –

A duet by guitarist Laurindo Almeida and studio singer Salli Terri. This song tells in a minute and a half of a broken-hearted woman instructing a Portuguese bluebird. Since the "sertão" (a desolate area of Brazil) mentioned in the lyric is unknown to most, this is my liberal English translation.

Fly little bluebird, my one true companion, go
And fly to my one love
Say that without him
My heart is no longer my heart, oh
Fly little bluebird
Go tell him, companion, go

❀ **SMILE** – *Charlie Chaplin, Thomas Beckmann (cellist)*

Charlie Chaplin wrote the melody to this hopeful song for his silent classic, *City Lights*. Again, music for both the departed and the audience.

❀ **TO KILL A MOCKINGBIRD** –

Elmer Bernstein & The Royal Philharmonic Pops Orchestra

This evocative theme from the movie gets an "A" for "admirably poignant." Even without linking it to some of the characters or the injustice done in the film or the events of a summer in one's life, it covers a lot of emotional ground.

REALIST

❀ **THE PARTY'S OVER** – *Jo Stafford*
Ah, but what a party it was.

ROMANTIC

❀ **AIN'T NO SUNSHINE** – *Bill Withers*
A song to put on the turntable while the ice cubes harden.

❀ **DEVOTED TO YOU** – *The Everly Brothers*
If you think she never really appreciated him, this is the
moment of the telling.

❀ **MOZART PIANO CONCERTO NO. 21,
SECOND MOVEMENT (ANDANTE)** –
Sir Neville Mariner: Academy of St. Martin in the Fields
For lovers from the '60s. This music was the score for a pop-
ular Swedish film, *Elvira Madigan*, where a beautiful blonde
tightrope walker falls in love with a soldier who has deserted
— either as an anti-war statement or for some of that good
Nordic booty.

For something to do while they're walking around the woods
eating berries, Elvira sets up a rope between two trees and does
her balancing act while the soundtrack plays Mozart's graceful
music. Then, as the couple realizes the futility of living in the
forest, starving from this mono-diet of loganberries, too tired to
make love, more of the dilemma unfolds: The soldier can't go
back to his regiment because he'll be jailed as a deserter, and if
the girl leaves she would be losing her true love. Two shots ring
out. We know the first is the guy shooting the girl. It's unclear
who took the second bullet. Most assume the soldier shot himself but maybe Elvira was just grazed and needed to be put out of
her misery. There's also the theory that an innocent little bunny
rabbit happened along and became dinner-for-one for Sven.

While the hippie movement perished due to a declining income stream based on black lights or tie-dye, Mozart's music lives on, even when we're not recalling beautiful tightrope walkers and idealistic soldiers.

❀ **MY FUNNY VALENTINE** – *Chet Baker*
A crystalline enigma of a song filled with seeming put-downs that lead to the highest of compliments.

❀ **SLEEPWALK** – *Santo & Johnny*
You probably know this dreamy song is an instrumental. Before hippies were hippies, they were innocent teenagers trying to dance close in the shadow of the older kids, the juvenile delinquents.

❀ **THESE FOOLISH THINGS** – *Billie Holiday*
If you're an incurable romantic and lost someone close to you, this song could be healing.

SENTIMENTAL

❀ **NEVERTHELESS** – *The Mills Brothers*
"Nevertheless" is poignant in a way that relates to couples and unrequited love. But don't rule out the element of surprise in using this song for a misanthrope or curmudgeon who finally saw the light.

❀ **THEME FROM CINEMA PARADISO** – *Soundtrack*
Music that speaks of time passed.

The main character in the film is a boy from a little Italian town who grows up to be a director. Raised by a mother whose husband was killed in WWII, he never marries. Later, as a successful filmmaker, he returns to his boyhood town for the funeral of his mentor and friend, Alfredo, who gave him his first job as projectionist at the Cinema Paradiso.

❀ **THEME FROM IL POSTINO** – *Soundtrack*
Short and sweet. A bandoneon (a type of concertina) plays the melody. Music for the love-struck.

SERIOUS

❀ **BRAHMS' SYMPHONY No. 3 in F, THIRD MOVEMENT** –
Various orchestras
An intensely moving melody — tragic and triumphant. As the
piece is over six minutes long, you may want to have it short-
ened.

❀ **IN MY LIFE** – *The Beatles*
If you are a dedicated Fab Four fan, you would want something played from their vast collection of published songs.
Make those blessed mourners weep as they reflect on how
much they were loved and thought of.

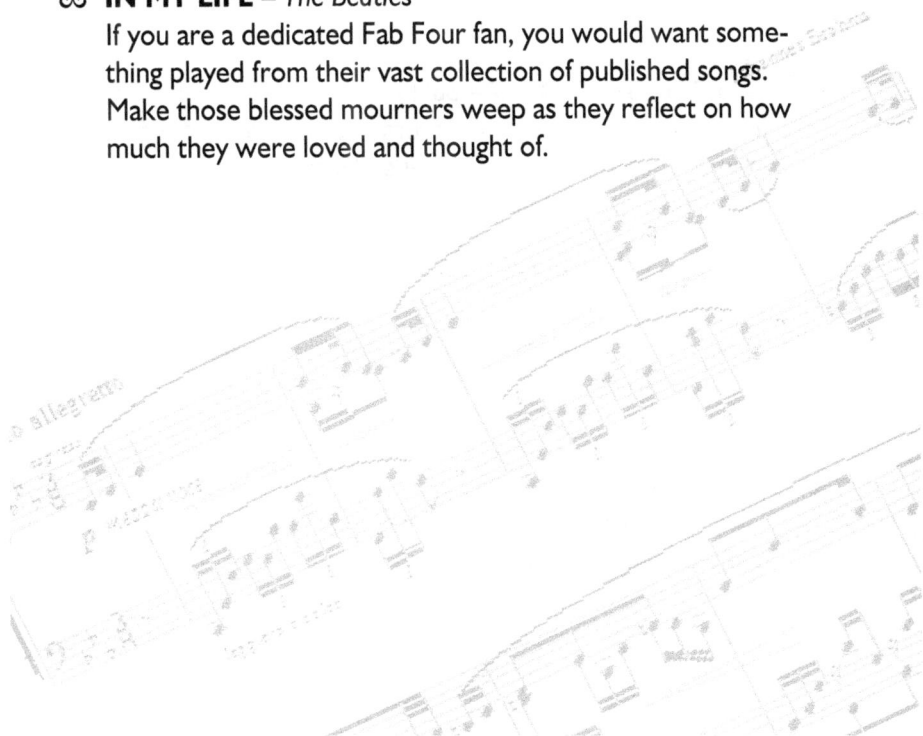

SHE'S GONE

❀ **HERE WITHOUT YOU** – *The Byrds*
A song that says everything about missing someone.

❀ **IN DREAMS** – *Roy Orbison*
Although this song became associated with the film *Blue Velvet*, it stands alone as a chilling testimony to the great beyond.

❀ **IT'S ALL OVER NOW** – *Bobby Womack, The Rolling Stones*
If you expect many former lovers to show up at your friend's memorial as in Francois Truffaut's *The Man Who Loved Women*, then you should have this song ready to go. The Stones did a fine job covering the tune, but consider the original recording by Bobby Womack.

Nothing says "finality" like "It's All Over Now." Reincarnators, blog your hearts out.

❀ **MISSING YOU** – *John Waite*
Take advantage of one of the most beautiful voices in rock. And the song works for either sex.

SINCERE

❀ **SENTIMENTAL JOURNEY** – *Fats Domino*

Most of the sincere people I knew were from my parent's WWII generation. They didn't find certain things funny because of their inherent sincerity; they eschewed foolishness. As a result, some of their children came away with a similar brand of seriousness. We called them "straight."

In the case of this song the audience is taking a sentimental journey, remembering their friend or relative's kindness and authenticity.

❀ **TURN! TURN! TURN!** – *The Byrds, Pete Seeger*

If you're the least little bit religious or philosophical, you can't go wrong with these words taken mostly from the Book of Ecclesiastes.

STATELY

✿ **EXCERPT FROM GUSTAV HOLST'S "JUPITER, THE BRINGER OF JOLLITY" FROM THE PLANETS –**
The Chicago Symphony Orchestra conducted by James Levine
When something like Elgar's overused "Pomp and Circumstance" is called for but you don't want to remind people of graduation exercises, this equally English-sounding melody will do the trick. Start at bar 184. There is no chord of finality so you'll have to fade the track or do some fancy editing at bar 233. I test-marketed this idea in 2000 and it worked out well.

STRAIGHT-OUT RELIGIOUS

❀ **OH HAPPY DAY** – *Edwin Hawkins Singers*
A gospel shouter. For those with soul.

❀ **RIVERS OF BABYLON** – *The Melodians*
Rasta or not, believers gather 'round.

SURFER

❀ **THE LONELY SURFER** –
Jack Nitzsche (and the Wrecking Crew), The Ventures
The original recording by composer-arranger Jack Nitzsche
is broad and majestic, but too much for a quiet goodbye. Try
the sparseness and introspection of the Venture's version.

❀ **SURFIN' BIRD** – *The Trashmen*
Picture your friend's life being celebrated by graying
skateboarders doing flips on ramps at the front of the church.

❀ **THINK ABOUT THE DAYS** – *The Beach Boys*
Music by the Beach Boys with no references to girls, cars, or
surfing; instead, we get a minute and a half of a cappella vocal
"ahs." Pure.

SURVIVALIST

❀ **I AM WAITING** – *The Rolling Stones*
For the Armageddon-averse who once lived in well-stocked hideaways.

SYMBOLIC-SPIRITUAL

❀ **ANGEL BABY** – *Rosie and the Originals*
Your friend strongly believed in an afterlife. The "you" in the song could be Jesus, Buddha, Krishna, or the concept of universal Oneness.

❀ **BEYOND THE BLUE HORIZON** – *Lou Christie*
If Roy Orbison's "In Dreams" is too slow, this peppy version of another classic song would serve for one who was active in life and reflective toward the end.

❀ **BRING IT ON HOME TO ME** – *Sam Cooke*
One song that bridged the gap between gospel and R&B.

❀ **GET BACK** – *The Beatles*
Perfect for those in attendance who share a belief in reincarnation or rejoining the eternal energy force. Beatles fan? Even better.

❀ **MASSA'S ON DE ROAD AGAIN** – *Franck und Jhaz*
A gospel rarity: "I see him waiting at bus stops/ He knows that life's a hard road/ He gives his seat to the people/ They leave him standing in the cold."

❀ **MICHAEL, ROW THE BOAT ASHORE** – *Pete Seeger*
Honor your friend with a performance by a great artist and human being.

❀ **TAKE ME TO THE RIVER** – *Al Green, Mavis Staples*
Again, for the "metaphoricals" in the audience who will instantly understand the deeper meaning of "river" as life flowing on, here are two versions in all their R&B and a cappella glory.

❀ **WE'LL MEET AGAIN** – *Vera Lynn, The Byrds*
An English song closely identified with WWII makes another case for reincarnation. Mozart is often mentioned in this regard as is the Dalai Lama. But do dogs return as people? Is your current golden retriever your late Aunt Gertie? When I accidentally stepped on a cockroach this morning, did I kill Hitler? As with all of metaphysics, no one really knows. If you and your guests believe — or would like to — this song will resonate.

THEY WENT AT THE SAME TIME

❀ **TOGETHER AGAIN** – *Buck Owens*
This song is good for two groups. For country music fans, it's a natural. If you're inclined to the metaphysical side of life, it also works as religious symbolism. And the fabulous hound dog-like pedal steel guitar instrumental is as good as it gets.

THOUGHTFUL

❀ **HAVING A CIGARETTE** – *Fate*
A quiet solo piano piece. Simple and reflective. A winding road.

❀ **LAY DOWN YOUR WEARY TUNE** – *Bob Dylan, The Byrds*
The struggle is over if that's what it was. No more contacts to maintain, no more appointments, no more baloney, no more missed opportunities. All that has passed. Now is peace.

❀ **NATURE BOY** – *Ella Fitzgerald*
All about love.

❀ **THE SOUNDS OF SILENCE** – *Simon and Garfunkle*
A song about the search for connection — needed more than ever.

❀ **THOSE WERE THE DAYS** – *Mary Hopkin*
A celebration of the past and where life led us.

U.F.O. BELIEVER

❀ **THE DAY THE EARTH STOOD STILL** –
(Prelude/Outer Space/Radar) - Soundtrack
Composer Bernard Herrmann captures the mystery of the
great beyond or, if you prefer, outer space.

❀ **AFTER THE GOLDRUSH** – *Prelude*
Just so there's no confusion, the name of the band is Prelude.
There is no instrumental backing to this Neil Young-written
song, just layered voices that capture innocence like fireflies
in a bottle. (No fireflies were harmed during the making of
this paragraph.)

VIETNAM VET

❀ **GOIN' DOWN SLOW** – Bobby "Blue" Bland
If this isn't a song for goodbyes, what is? "Goin' Down Slow" builds lyrically and musically — starting off with a small rhythm section and lead vocal, ending up five and a half minutes later with spitty horns and gospel-inspired singers.

❀ **WILLIAM SCHUMAN'S "SYMPHONY FOR STRINGS"**
SYMPHONY No. 5 – I Musici de Montreal & Yuli Torovsky
Twentieth century classical music can be beautiful for some and painful for others. A goodbye underscored with dissonance.

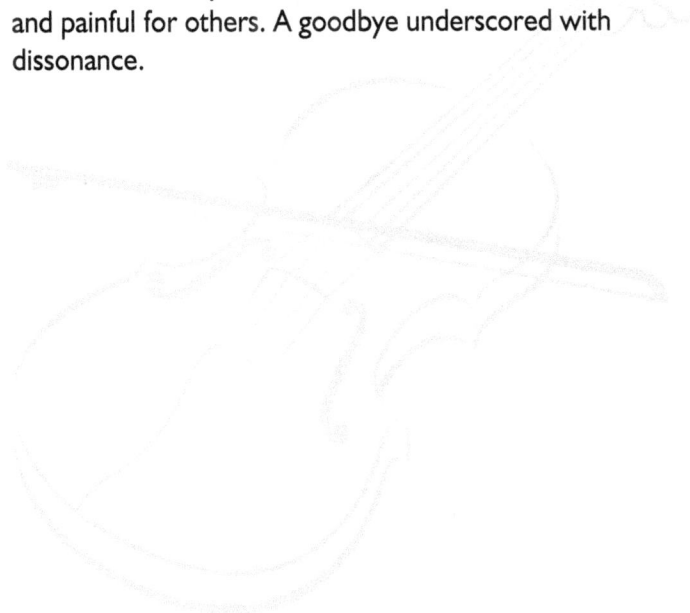

ZANY OR MISCELLANY

❀ **HIGH ANXIETY** –
Mel Brooks (with the John Morris Orchestra)
As with the earlier Mel Brooks-penned recommendation,
the theme from *Blazing Saddles*, you'll need to know your
audience. This may be one of the funniest songs ever written,
well performed by the writer himself.

❀ **YES, I'M READY** – *Barbara Mason*
Ready to meet the Maker.

Self-expression is one of the qualities that lights up the sky when we think of baby boomers — tie-dye comes to mind — so some of us boom booms might prefer to choose our own special music for that final goodbye scene where Shane or Shania rides off into the sinking sun.

With that scenario in mind,
here's what I want played at my going-away party:

Pre-service seating music:
*Missa In Festo Pentecostes by The Nuns' Choir of the
Benedictine Abbey of Our Lady of Varensell (out of print).
Gregorian chant may be an unusual way to start the service but
this is simply beautiful music.*

Before the moderator begins speaking,
play the following edited songs:

Cut 1: "Nevertheless"– *The Mills Brothers, from 0:00 to 1:40*
Cut 2: "Goin' Down Slow" – *Bobby "Blue" Bland, from 0:00 to 0:47*
Cut 3: "Azulão" – *Laurindo Almeida and Salli Terri, 0:41 to 1:26*
Cut 4: "Love is Alive" – *Gary Wright, 0:50 to 1:18, fade from 1:09 to 1:18*
Cut 5: "Eensy Weensy Spider" – *The Cedarmont Kids, from 0:28 to 0:53*
Cut 6: "Together Again" – *Buck Owens, from 0:50 to 2:25*
Cut 7: "Sam, The Old Accordion Man" – *The Williams Sisters,
0:00 to 1:58, fade from 1:58 to 2:04*

Exit music: *"Having a Cigarette" by Fate*

Title	Writer(s)
A Whiter Shade of Pale	G. Brooker, K. Reid, M. Fisher
After the Goldrush	Neil Young
Ain't No Sunshine	Bill Withers
All Right Now	Paul Rodgers
Also sprach Zarathustra	Richard Strauss
Angel Baby	Rosie Hamlin
Azulão	M. Bandeira, J. Ovalle
Baba O'Riley	Pete Townshend
Because	John Lennon, Paul McCartney
Beyond the Blue Horizon	Harlan Howard, Hank Cochran
Black Is Black	M. Grainger, T. Hayes, S. Wadley
Blazing Saddles	Mel Brooks, John Morris
Born to Be Wild	Mars Bonfire
Brahms' Symphony No. 3	Johannes Brahms
Bring It On Home to Me	Sam Cooke
Cast Your Fate to the Wind	Vince Guaraldi
Devoted to You	Felice & Boudleaux Bryant
Don't Bother Me	George Harrison
Feeling Good	Leslie Bricusse, Anthony Newley
Get Back	John Lennon, Paul McCartney

Title   Writer(s)

Title	Writer(s)

Title	**Writer(s)**
Whip It	Gerald Casale, Mark Mothersbaugh
White Rabbit	Grace Slick
Wild Weekend	Tom Shannon, Phil Todaro
Wildfire	M. Murphey, L. Cansler
Windy	Ruthann Friedman
Yes, I'm Ready	Barbara Mason
You're No Good	Clint Ballard Jr.
You've Let Yourself Go	Charles Aznavour

NOTES

FIN